Before the Ring

A Successful Family Resource Guide

Dr. Creflo A. Dollar and Taffi L. Dollar

Before the Ring: Resource Guide
ISBN 1-59089-699-8
Copyright © 2002 by Dr. Creflo A. Dollar and Taffi L. Dollar

Published by Creflo Dollar Ministries
P.O. Box 490124
College Park, GA 30349

CONTENTS

HOW TO USE THIS RESOURCE GUIDE

Strong individuals make strong families. That is why this resource guide is a vital element in *The Successful Family* series. When used in conjunction with *Part I: Before the Ring*, of *The Successful Family* reference book, this guide becomes a dynamic tool that will assist you in achieving the success you desire in your relationships. It is a good idea to read and sign the commitment certificate in this guide before beginning your journey to a successful family.

There is no right or wrong way to use this guide. You may complete the exercises alone, with a partner or in a group. However, be sure to allow enough time to review the relevant chapters and complete the corresponding exercises. Don't give up if an exercise seems challenging. Press your way through, and ask someone for help, if necessary. Remember, your goal is to see what areas of your life need to be changed, and then make the appropriate adjustment with the Word of God.

Follow these steps to prepare for each exercise:

- Pray for wisdom
- Read the corresponding chapter(s) in part one of *The Successful Family*
- Complete the exercise(s)

- Apply what you learn to your life

For every problem there is a solution. You can make the most of your single life and become a solution-oriented person by studying the biblical principles in each exercise. And don't forget to enjoy the journey to successful, vibrant relationships!

MY COMMITMENT

If you are fed up with failed relationships and are serious about seeing change take place in your life, read the following statements and then sign your name at the bottom of this page. Make time in your daily schedule to give voice to your commitment to change so that you can remain focused.

- I will read *Part I: Before the Ring*, of *The Successful Family* and complete the corresponding exercises. If this is a group session, and I must miss a meeting, I will make up all missed assignments.
- I will designate a specific time frame daily in which to study the information and complete the exercises.
- If this is a group, I will be on time for each session. I realize that my tardiness is a distraction to others and causes me to miss out on valuable information.
- I will share my answers with a trusted friend and/or participate in group discussions.
- I will be honest with myself and/or other group members.
- I commit to love myself enough to successfully complete this session no matter how difficult or challenging the exercises seem.

- I will apply what I learn and periodically gauge my growth.
- I commit to confidentiality and will not discuss the personal affairs of others outside of the group.

_____

Signature   Date

Exercise One:

YOU ARE SPECIAL!

To be *single* means, "to be separate, unique and whole." No one in the world will ever be just like you. You have very distinct qualities! Think about that for a moment. What makes you, you? Is it the way you laugh, dress or look? What about the things you say and the way in which you process information? Think about the characteristics and qualities that make you a unique person. List 10 of them here.

1._____

2._____

3._____

4._____

5._____

6._____

7._____

8._____

9._____

10._____

On those days when you need an emotional boost, look at the qualities you have listed, and remember that you are a one-of-a-kind creation, precious in God's sight!

ME, MYSELF AND I

Complete the following statements. Write down the first thing that comes to mind as you read each one. You may wish to keep the answers to yourself or share them with a good friend, your intended or the group leader. In addition, consider asking one of the aforementioned people to reveal how they see you by completing the exercise and sharing their responses with you. This will assist you in gaining even more insight into your personality!

1. I see myself as_____

_____

2. Three words that best describe me are_____

_____

3. I am at my best when _____

_____

4. I am at my worst when_____

_____

5. My best quality is_____

_____

6. My worst quality is_____

_____

7. I am strongest when_____

_____

8. I am weakest when_____

_____

9. I become quiet when_____

_____

10. My feelings tend to be hurt when_____

_____

11. I believe others view me as_____

_____

12. You could say that my relationship with God is_____

because_____

13. I get angry when_____

_____

14. When I get angry with someone, I tend to_____

_____

15. I love it when_____

_____

16. I feel inadequate when_____

_____

17. My family and I_____

_____

18. My past dating experience has been_____

_____

19. I think I am a "good catch" because_____

_____

20. My greatest desire in life is to_____

_____

HOW SINGLE ARE YOU?

Are you content in your singleness, or do you continually strive to "complete" yourself by becoming romantically involved with others? Are you making the most of your single life or just "killing time" until you find "the one?" There is a difference between being single and being alone. To be *single* implies who you are; it means that you don't need anyone else to make you feel like a "whole" person. To be *alone* describes the state you're in: by yourself. Although Adam was alone in the Garden of Eden, he didn't feel incomplete. He was content in his singleness. God created Eve as an added benefit.

The following test is designed to help you see where you are in your singleness and enable you to enhance this period of time in your life. Answer each question by circling your answer. Then tally your score to see how content you are as a single person.

1. I strive to change personal habits that annoy others, except for those habits that are important to me.
   (a) Usually   (b) Often   (c) Occasionally   (d) Rarely

2. I seek to promote the needs of others over my own needs.
   (a) Usually   (b) Often   (c) Occasionally   (d) Rarely

3. I am content to be without a mate or a steady date.
    (a) Usually   (b) Often   (c) Occasionally   (d) Rarely

4. I don't need a partner to add meaning to my life.
    (a) Usually   (b) Often   (c) Occasionally   (d) Rarely

5. I am happy for my friends when they get married.
    (a) Usually   (b) Often   (c) Occasionally   (d) Rarely

6. I don't mind when my partner (or friends) asks for space.
    (a) Usually   (b) Often   (c) Occasionally   (d) Rarely

7. I am not offended when my partner (or friends) do not respond to sit
    uations as I do.
    (a) Usually   (b) Often   (c) Occasionally   (d) Rarely

8. I believe that spending quality time with God is essential to my over-
    all well-being.
    (a) Usually   (b) Often   (c) Occasionally   (d) Rarely

Allow 3 points for every "a" and "b" answer and 1 point for every "c" and "d" answer.

20–24: You seem to understand your position as a single person in Christ Jesus. You know that true happiness stems from a vibrant, personal relationship with God and seek companionship from those who are content in their singleness. Remember, the secret to enjoying life as a single person is to love yourself for who you are and keep your relationship with Jesus strong and vibrant.

18-16: You are still working toward grasping the concept of being complete in Christ. Continue to focus on your relationship with God so that He can continue to reveal the characteristics that make you special and unique to Him. Keep in mind that true intimacy with God is built over time and by open and honest communication with Him.

14-8: You are having difficulty being content in your singleness. To resolve this issue, put first things first. The best solution is to work on yourself and your relationship with God, *then* establish healthy friendships with others. It doesn't work the other way around!

Make it a point to enjoy your individuality by allowing your uniqueness to complement those with whom you establish close relationships. Once you come to the realization that being single is healthy, you will avoid future heartache and pave the way for a successful marriage!

Exercise Four:

THE ROAD TO SINGLE-MINDEDNESS

Answer the following questions using chapter one of *The Successful Family* as a guide. After writing down your responses, take a few moments to reflect on how your beliefs influence your life as a single person.

1. God says that it's okay to be single. To be *single* means, "to be separate, unique and whole." What do those qualities mean to you?_____

_____

_____

_____

How does this influence your thinking?_____

_____

_____

_____

2. Why isn't it a good thing to become involved with individuals who are not content in their singleness?_____

_____

_____

_____

How does this influence your thinking?_____

_____

_____

_____

3.   Being *single* is different from being *alone*. How do they differ? What does it mean to be *alone?* What can you do to keep from feeling that way?_____

_____

_____

_____

How does this influence your thinking?_____

_____

_____

_____

4.   What did God mean in Genesis 2:18 when He said He was making a "help meet" for Adam? _____

_____

_____

_____

How does this influence your thinking?_____

_____

_____

_____

5.   Why is the statement, "God chose that person just for me," not a true statement?_____

_____

_____

_____

How does this influence your thinking?_____

_____

_____

_____

Exercise Five:

IT'S ALL IN THE PRESENTATION

Over the course of time God will make several presentations to you for a mate. Although having to choose one person out of many may seem overwhelming, remember that God is willing to help you choose the best person for you. In fact, He has outlined several prerequisites for a mate in 2 Corinthians 6:14-18. Write out those verses below.

_____

_____

_____

_____

_____

_____

_____

_____

_____

_____

_____

Using these scriptures as a guideline, make a list of the character-istics and places that *would be* a part of God's presentation.

1._____

2._____

3._____

4._____

5._____

Using these scriptures as a guideline, make a list of the character-istics and places that *would not* be a part of God's presentation.

1._____

2._____

3._____

4._____

5._____

Always base your decisions on the Word of God. When you make it the final authority in your life, you position yourself to receive wisdom; therefore, you won't be confused about God's presentations to you!

Exercise Six:

SAY GOOD-BYE TO THE DATING GAME

What does God think about dating? Does it matter to Him who we date or how often we go out with someone? Dating was designed as the *getting to know you* period in a couple's relationship before marriage. Although "dating" isn't specifically mentioned in the Bible, there are definite guidelines throughout Proverbs and the New Testament that, when followed, will lead you into a healthy relationship and enable you to choose a life partner wisely. Therefore, don't waste valuable time on something temporary or settle for second best!

Take a moment to think about your past dating relationships, then answer the following questions.

1. Why is a person's character impotant?_____

_____

_____

_____

_____

_____

2. How does worldly dating differ from Christian dating?_____

_____

_____

_____

_____

_____

3. Why is fornication wrong?_____

_____

_____

_____

_____

_____

4. What are some healthy dating guidelines?_____

_____

_____

_____

_____

_____

SOMEONE TO WATCH OVER ME

Under the headings below, write down the characteristics that you are looking for in a potential mate, keeping in mind the prerequisites outlined in 2 Corinthians 6:14-18. Use one block for each characteristic. Afterward, look up and list the scriptures that back up what you've written down. Confess them aloud several times daily. In addition, use your list as a guide for selecting a spouse after a presentation has been made!

SPIRITUAL	PHYSICAL	EMOTIONAL	INTELLECTUAL	OPTIONAL

SPIRITUAL	PHYSICAL	EMOTIONAL	INTELLECTUAL	OPTIONAL

TRUE LOVE OR TRUE LUST?

Read each sentence below and determine whether it is true or false. Circle your answer. When you are finished, compare your answers to the answer key at the end of this guide.

1. People who believe in "love at first sight" often blind   T   F
   themselves to the shortcomings of others.

2. Sincerity is the foundation for a romantic and   T   F
   fulfilling relationship.

3. Sex is the only way to show how much you really care   T   F
   for someone.

4. Physical attraction is not a bad thing.   T   F

5. Christians should only date someone who they believe   T   F
   is a suitable candidate for marriage.

6. A healthy, "romantic" relationship can only be built on   T   F
   the foundation of friendship.

7. It is all right to indulge in heavy kissing and petting   T   F
   after you are engaged to be married.

8. When people fornicate (have sex before marriage),   T   F
   they violate a spiritual law.

9. Fornication can create a negative soul tie and change   T   F
    one's personality.

10. When you have sex with a person, you are also   T   F
    having sex with everyone in their sexual history.

11. You can be very attracted to someone and remain   T   F
    sexually pure.

12. If you date someone with the intention of having   T   F
    fun now and then breaking off the relationship later,
    you are actually practicing divorce.

13. Being single is a curse.   T   F

Exercise Nine:

A STUDY IN PROVERBS

You can avoid the most common dating pitfalls by making the Word of God the final authority in every area of your life. This means aligning your thoughts and actions with what it says. Proverbs 7 gives believers specific warnings regarding wrong relationships between men and women.

As you read the verses in this chapter, write down your thoughts about what they are saying and how you can apply their principles to your dating life.

Verses1-4_____

_____

_____

_____

Verse 5_____

_____

_____

_____

Verse 6-7_____

_____

_____

_____

Verses 8-9_____

_____

_____

_____

Verse 10_____

_____

_____

_____

Verses 11-12_____

_____

_____

_____

Verses 13-20_____

_____

_____

_____

Verse 21_____

_____

_____

_____

Verses 22-23_____

_____

_____

_____

Verses 24-25_____

_____

_____

_____

Verses 26-27_____

_____

_____

_____

Exercise Ten:

HOW CREATIVE!

The time you spend with your friends or on a date doesn't have to be boring; instead, it can be a downright adventure!

The activities listed below have been divided into several groups, ranging from expensive to inexpensive and from daring to tame. Some can be done in a day, others over several days. Grab a few friends and try one or more of these diversions, then rate them on a scale of 1 to 10 (with 1 being "never again" and 10 being "worth repeating").

Keep in mind that change is a positive thing. Don't be afraid to try something you've never done before! You never know—depending on the size of your wallet (and the strength of your backbone), you may discover a hidden talent, take up a new hobby or make new friends!

Expensive/Daring	Moderate/Daring	Inexpensive/Daring
Shark Feeding	Skydiving	Bungee Jumping
Big Game Hunting	Rollercoaster Marathon	Tightrope Walking
Mountain Climbing	White-Water Rafting	Volcano Exploration
Hot Air Ballooning	Ride in a Stunt Plane	Spelunking
Photo Safari (Africa/India)	Parasailing	Rock Wall Climbing and Rappelling

Expensive/Tame	Moderate/Tame	Inexpensive/Tame
Dinner at the Ritz	Dinner Theatre	Karaoke Singing
Helicopter Ride	Dance Lessons	Rollerblading
Swim With Dolphins	Sporting Event	Museum/Historic Sight
Rent a Yacht	Horseback Riding	Play a Board Game
Spa Weekend	Water Skiing	Rent a Movie

Here are several other ideas you may wish to try!

Expensive	Moderate	Inexpensive
Dinner in Another Major City	Play Arcade Video Games	Picnic
Ride the Orient Express	Visit a Theme Park	Fishing
Take a Cruise	Horse-Drawn Carriage Ride	Swing Dancing
SCUBA Diving	Go-Cart Racing	Ice Skating

ARE YOU A GENTLEMAN?

Every man should understand the importance of being a gentleman and of meeting the basic needs of a woman. If you miss the core reasons for why you should treat a lady well, then your actions will remain superficial.

Listed below are the five basic needs of women. Under each need are several examples of how you can meet it. On a scale of 1 – 5 (with 1 being the lowest and 5 the highest), consider how often you do these things and then rate yourself in each category.

Need: Affection	**Rating**
You call her just to say, "I love you."	_____
You send her a card or flowers for no reason.	_____
You pull out the chair for her at a restaurant.	_____
You open doors for her and help her with her coat.	_____
You compliment her regularly.	_____
You hold her hand while walking or hug her for no reason.	_____

Need: Communication   Rating

You share with her what has happened
in your day.   _____

You refrain from predicting what she is
going to say.   _____

You don't ridicule her concerns.   _____

You try to be receptive to her point of view. _____

You don't expect her to read your mind. _____

You share your thoughts and feelings with her. _____

Need: Honesty and Openness   Rating

When you are wrong, you quickly apologize. _____

You do not allow pride or fear to keep you
from being open.   _____

You do not allow insecurity to keep you
from being honest.   _____

You open up to her because you trust her. _____

You don't try to be someone you are not. _____

When asked a question, you answer truthfully. _____

Need: Financial Support   Rating

When on a date, you always pay.   _____

You fill her gas tank. _____

You buy something for her when
it's least expected. _____

You always look for ways to give,
regardless of the budget. _____

You've discussed financial issues with her. _____

You mutually agree on financial
responsibility/accountability. _____

Need: Family Commitment   Rating

You are cautious about appearances
with the opposite sex. _____

You never compare her to another woman. _____

You find out what's important to her
and support her in it. _____

You never give her a reason to be jealous
of another woman. _____

You spend time with her instead
of your buddies. _____

You are always there when
she needs you. _____

Your Score

If you gave yourself a **5** or a **4** after each statement, keep up the good work! If you gave yourself a **3**, your romancing could use a boost. Concentrate your energy on the area(s) that needs the most improvement without neglecting the area(s) in which you received a high score. If you scored mostly **2s** or **1s**, you need a real overhaul! What is hindering you from meeting the basic needs of the woman in your life? Is it fear, pride or a lack of knowledge? Whatever the case may be, do your best to uncover the problem and then remedy the situation.

Exercise Twelve:

ACTIONS SPEAK LOUDER

Ephesians 5:25 states, *"Husbands, love your wives, even as Christ also loved the church, and gave himself for it."* This principle applies to you, even if you are single. How? If you want to marry, you must learn early on how to love your future spouse as Christ loves you.

Think of the ways in which you can enhance your skills in meeting the five basic needs—affection, communication, honesty and openness, financial support and family commitment—of your future bride. Write down your ideas/goals beside each heading. For example, under the *communication* heading you may write, "I will share more details about my day with my girlfriend/fiancée this week."

1. In the area of *affection*, I will begin to _____

_____

_____

_____

2. In the area of *communication*, I will begin to_____

_____

_____

_____

3. In the area of *honesty* and *openness*, I will begin to_____

_____

_____

_____

4. In the area of *financial support*, I will begin to_____

_____

_____

_____

5. In the area of *family commitment*, I will begin to_____

_____

_____

_____

You may wish to tackle one area before beginning work in another, or just practice all areas at once. Set small goals each week and work toward accomplishing each one. Before long, your goals will have become habits!

REDEEM THE PAST

Dating and marriage are not quick fixes for personal problems; in fact, they can actually make a negative situation worse because they cannot fulfill any unmet needs stemming from childhood or adolescence. Almost every person lacks one or more positive qualities, such as good communication skills, the ability to set and enforce personal boundaries, or to maintain a healthy level of self-esteem and a positive self-image. This is often the result of one or both parents not meeting your needs, or from some other negative event that may have scarred you.

Although dating or marrying the right person can fulfill certain needs, you should never look to another person to make you feel complete. That longing can only be fulfilled through God and a personal relationship with Jesus Christ. Take a moment to reflect on your relationship with your parents. Write down the needs that you feel were not adequately met, or the negative events that shaped the way you think and feel. Putting these thoughts on paper will enable you to identify your needs and allow God to meet them in order to make you whole.

A LADY IN WAITING

Being a woman in this day and age isn't easy. The challenges of daily living often make it difficult to live by biblical values and high ethical standards. It is important for a woman to completely understand herself and her place in relationships. This comes only by the renewing of the mind with the Word of God. Before you can establish a successful relationship with another person, you must first understand how precious you are.

Proverbs 31 is a scriptural illustration of a woman's value. In the exercise below, write out what each verse means to you. Then begin to examine the areas in your life where you've not valued yourself. Work on those areas by changing the way in which you think, speak and act. As you immerse yourself in God's presence, you position yourself to walk confidently as a person of integrity and character. It is only through your relationship with God that you can mature as a woman and experience His best in your life.

Verse 10 means_____

_____

_____

_____

After meditating on this scripture, I will begin to_____

_____

_____

_____

Verses 11-12 mean _____

_____

_____

_____

After meditating on these scriptures, I will begin to_____

_____

_____

_____

Verses 13-21 mean _____

_____

_____

_____

After meditating on these scriptures, I will begin to _____

_____

_____

_____

Verses 22-25 mean _____

_____

_____

_____

After meditating on these scriptures, I will begin to_____

_____

_____

_____

Verse 26 means _____

_____

_____

_____

After meditating on this scripture, I will begin to_____

_____

_____

Verses 27-31 mean _____

_____

_____

_____

After meditating on these scriptures, I will begin to _____

_____

_____

_____

Exercise Fifteen:

THE ROAD LESS TRAVELED

Look at the chart below. Across the top are six numbers that correspond to six questions. Read question 1. Now look at column 1. On a scale of 1 to 8 (with 8 being the highest—"I *never* do this," or "I would *never* feel this way" and 1 being the lowest—"I *always* do this," or "I *always* feel this way"), rate yourself. Once you have answered the questions, draw a line between the numbers you have circled.

1	2	3	4	5	6
8	8	8	8	8	8
7	7	7	7	7	7
6	6	6	6	6	6
5	5	5	5	5	5
4	4	4	4	4	4
3	3	3	3	3	3
2	2	2	2	2	2
1	1	1	1	1	1

1. If my friend doesn't want to come over, I start to cry and complain of loneliness.

2. I allow my friends to make fun of me.

3. I settle for anyone because the choices are slim.

4. My friends have a way of talking me out of sticking to my principles.

5. If I don't dress in a sexy manner, I won't attract the opposite sex.

6. The older I get, the less likely my chances are of meeting "the one."

Notice the line you have drawn. Is it jagged or smooth? How jagged is your road of self-value? Do you think highly of yourself, or do you possess low self-esteem and settle for whatever comes your way?

HOW MUCH DO YOU REALLY KNOW?

Read each incomplete statement below. Circle the answer that best completes each sentence. When you are finished, compare your responses with those in the answer key at the end of this resource guide.

1. Proverbs 13:20 states that those who fellowship with wise people will_____.
    (a) be rich   (b) be wise   (c) be entertained   (d) be holy

2. To ensure that someone would make a good friend, you should_____.
    (a) ask about his or her income   (b) listen to the words that are spoken
    (c) see if you share common interests (d) hang out with him/her for a few
                                                  weeks

3. You can experience successful relationships by aligning yourself with_____.
    (a) God's Word   (b) the planets
    (c) The Holy Spirit's direction   (d) your church beliefs

4. A good man will_____.
    (a) esteem you highly   (b) be unemployed and watch TV all
                                             day
    (c) shower you with gifts   (d) be faithful

5. Just as an insect is attracted to the petals of a flower, so, too, are men attracted to a woman who _____.
    (a) wears nice perfume   (b) maintains her physical appearance
    (c) talks in a loud voice   (d) dresses for success

6. What a woman is willing to show, makes a man think she is _____.
   (a) proud of her body   (b) conceited
   (c) willing to change   (d) willing to share

7. The best way to show a man that you love him is by _____.
   (a) preparing a candlelight dinner   (b) washing his clothes
   (c) encouraging him   (d) being affectionate

8. When you have trouble with your partner, it is best to_____.
   (a) stop immediately and pray   (b) seek wise council
   (c) make your point quickly   (d) talk to your friends about the issue

9. A woman who values herself_____.
   (a) is rare   (b) submits to authority
   (c) is faithful   (d) sees herself as God sees her

10. Men base their success on what they have achieved, while women base their success on_____.
    (a) what they create   (b) what they endure
    (c) their level of adaptability   (d) the strength of their relationships

TEST YOUR KNOWLEDGE

Read each statement below and determine whether it is true (T) or false (F). When you are finished, check your answers with those in the answer key at the back of this guide.

1. It is important for a woman to understand herself and her place in a relationship.   **T**   **F**

2. If a woman's mind is not renewed, she might try to secure a relationship through false impressions, manipulation or sex.   **T**   **F**

3. You should never stay in a relationship just to keep from being alone.   **T**   **F**

4. The relationship you compromise to keep is the one you will lose.   **T**   **F**

5. Most men are called to do specific things, but a woman has a pool of abilities from which she can draw and do many things.   **T**   **F**

6. Women of value do not chase after men.   **T**   **F**

7. An intimate relationship with God is the key to maturity.   **T**   **F**

8. Purposeful women choose to participate in   **T**   **F**

productive and encouraging conversations.

9. There's nothing wrong with showing a little skin, T   F
    especially in summer.

10. A woman who respects herself commands respect T   F
    from others.

Exercise Eighteen:

EVALUATE YOUR ASSETS AND LIABILITIES

On a scale of 1 to 5, (with 1 being the lowest and 5 the highest) rate yourself in the following areas. For example, if you are a very confident person, give yourself a 5 beside that trait. When finished, ask your partner to rate him/herself, using the same scale.

Once you have filled in your respective columns, subtract the numbers and place the answer in the column marked "Difference." Take special note of the areas that have more than a two-point difference. Be sure to discuss these areas in detail and work to improve your scores so that your future marriage will be a success

TENDENCIES	YOU	PARTNER		DIFFERENCE
Penny-pincher	____	____	=	____
Spendthrift	____	____	=	____
Passive	____	____	=	____
Aggressive	____	____	=	____
Confident	____	____	=	____
Affectionate	____	____	=	____
Open	____	____	=	____
Jealous	____	____	=	____

TENDENCIES	YOU	PARTNER		DIFFERENCE
Neat	_____	_____	=	_____
Punctual	_____	_____	=	_____
Dependable	_____	_____	=	_____
Helpful	_____	_____	=	_____
Assertive	_____	_____	=	_____
Workaholic	_____	_____	=	_____
Spiritual	_____	_____	=	_____
Decisive	_____	_____	=	_____
Hospitable	_____	_____	=	_____
Forgiving	_____	_____	=	_____
Teachable	_____	_____	=	_____
Flexible	_____	_____	=	_____
Mannerly/Polite	_____	_____	=	_____

Exercise Nineteen:

YOU'RE THE ONE

Marriage is not something that should be entered into lightly or in a hurry. It is a covenant, or agreement, that bonds two people together for life.

Have you taken enough time to really think through your reasons for wanting to marry your intended? List 10 of those reasons below.

1. _____

_____

_____

2. _____

_____

_____

3. _____

_____

_____

4. _____

_____

_____

5. _____

_____

_____

6. _____

_____

_____

7. _____

_____

_____

8. _____

_____

_____

9. _____

_____

_____

10. _____

_____

_____

What confirmation do you and your intended have that God has called you to join your lives together as one? Write the answer in the space below. You may wish to discuss this with your partner first, or complete the activity alone and share your answer(s) later.

Exercise Twenty:

COUPLE'S INVENTORY

1. How long have you known one another?_____

2. How did you meet? Where? When?_____

_____

_____

_____

_____

3. Did the presentation of your partner violate any of the prerequisites listed in 2 Corinthians 6:14-18?_____

_____

_____

_____

4. What attracted you to your partner?_____

_____

_____

_____

5. What made you decide to marry this person?_____

_____

_____

_____

6. Have you communicated this desire to your parents? How do they

feel about it?

_____

_____

_____

_____

7. What qualities does he/she possess that will enhance your marriage

relationship?

_____

_____

_____

_____

8. What were some of the topics discussed before you decided to marry?

_____

_____

_____

_____

9. Do you think there is anything that you have yet to discuss? What is it?_____

_____

_____

_____

10. What are the strong points in your relationship?_____

_____

_____

_____

11. What are the weak points?_____

_____

_____

_____

12. How have you begun to work on those weak points?_____

_____

_____

_____

13. Have you both reached the same level of spiritual maturity? Do you both have the same spiritual goals? What are they?_____

_____

_____

_____

14. Since the two of you have been together, have there been any hindrances to those goals? If so, how did you remedy the problem?_____

_____

_____

_____

15. Do you know how your partner was raised? How will the patterns he/she learned in childhood and adolescence influence your marriage?____

_____

_____

_____

16.   How will the way in which you were raised influence your marriage?

_____

_____

_____

_____

Exercise Twenty-One:

LOVE: A MANY SPLENDORED THING

On a scale of 1 to 3 (with 3 being the highest and 1 the lowest), rate your ability to love unconditionally. Answer each question honestly. After you have completed the exercise, go back and evaluate your partner. When you are finished, ask that person to take the test.

ATTRIBUTES	YOU	YOUR PARTNER
I am patient.	3 2 1	3 2 1
I am kind.	3 2 1	3 2 1
I maintain a positive outlook.	3 2 1	3 2 1
I am never jealous.	3 2 1	3 2 1
I am not anxious.	3 2 1	3 2 1
I am never envious.	3 2 1	3 2 1
I am never boastful or prideful.	3 2 1	3 2 1
I am not arrogant or conceited.	3 2 1	3 2 1
I am not rude.	3 2 1	3 2 1
I am not indecent.	3 2 1	3 2 1
I am never selfish.	3 2 1	3 2 1
I am not self-seeking.	3 2 1	3 2 1
I do not insist on having my way.	3 2 1	3 2 1

ATTRIBUTES	YOU	YOUR PARTNER
I am not quick to take offense.	3 2 1	3 2 1
I am not resentful.	3 2 1	3 2 1
I am not touchy or irritable.	3 2 1	3 2 1
I do not hold grudges.	3 2 1	3 2 1
I take no pleasure in wrongdoing.	3 2 1	3 2 1
I do not gloat over the failures of others.	3 2 1	3 2 1
I side with truth.	3 2 1	3 2 1
I am not dishonest.	3 2 1	3 2 1
I am open and transparent.	3 2 1	3 2 1
I overlook faults in others.	3 2 1	3 2 1
I have unquenchable faith.	3 2 1	3 2 1
My endurance is limitless.	3 2 1	3 2 1
I am eager to believe the best.	3 2 1	3 2 1
I always trust.	3 2 1	3 2 1
I always hope.	3 2 1	3 2 1
I always persevere.	3 2 1	3 2 1

Now compare your scores. In what ways will your ability or inability to love your partner affect your marriage? Were there areas in which you disagreed? Encourage one another to strengthen the traits with the lowest scores while maintaining those with high ratings.

Exercise Twenty-Two:

M. F. E. O. (MADE FOR EACH OTHER)

Circle the answer that best completes each of the sentences below.

1. It's not a good idea to marry someone just like you because _____.

   (a) you don't like yourself
   (c) weaknesses must be exchanged
       for strengths

   (b) *someone* needs to be rich
   (d) opposites attract

2. It's not wise to jump into marriage without first having _____.

   (a) lengthy conversations
   (c) using your partner's credit card

   (b) good sex
   (d) an engagement ring

3. You'll know your partner is born again if _____.

   (a) he/she comes from the South
   (c) he/she talks about God

   (b) he/she has been baptized
   (d) he/she has accepted Jesus
       as Lord and Savior

4. When the Bible warns against being "unequally yoked," it's speaking of _____.

   (a) a person's race
   (c) spiritual compatibility

   (b) not liking the same things
   (d) a difference of opinion

5. To find out if marriage is an option with your partner, you must _____.

   (a) see how he/she looks in a swimsuit
   (c) have great sex

   (b) ask questions
   (d) pick a fight

6. The wedding ceremony is _____.

   (a) a celebration
   (c) the time to voice the terms
       of marriage

   (b) very expensive
   (d) unnecessary

7. Submitting to a man is a huge commitment. That's why a woman must _____.

(a) know her fiancé well   (b) be on her guard

(c) have no real personality   (d) voice her opinion before marriage

8. Strong marriages begin with _____.

(a) strong in-laws   (b) strong bank accounts

(c) strong individuals   (d) desires and opinions

9. The best reason for marriage lies in _____.

(a) the woman's biological clock   (b) the man's libido

(c) a surprise pregnancy   (d) your willingness to commit yourself to another

10. *Submission* means_____.

(a) to get under someone's mission   (b) to become a doormat

(c) to hear from God   (d) to obey God's commands

Exercise Twenty-Three:

ON THE RIGHT FOOT

Your wedding day is a special time for both you and your intended. Although the proposal and acceptance may have only taken a few moments, planning for your big day can take up to 12 months! Listed below are a few topics you may wish to discuss with one another and your parents before contacting vendors and making financial obligations.

1. What kind of wedding do you want?

Once you are engaged, it is a good idea to sit down and discuss the type of wedding celebration you want. For instance, would you prefer a traditional ceremony or one with a more eclectic feel? How large or expensive will it be? Would you like the ceremony and/or reception to be indoors or out? Are there any special ethnic or religious customs you would like to incorporate? What about a theme or specific colors? Write down your ideas before committing to any one in particular. Bridal magazines, the Internet and former brides are good sources of information.

2. How will your parents contribute to your wedding?

Traditionally, the parents of the bride pay for their daughter's wedding, while the groom and his parents foot the bill for the rehearsal dinner, bridal bouquet and honeymoon. Today, it is common to see the bride and groom paying for their own wedding or both sets of parents contributing to the overall cost. After you are engaged, sit down with your parents and discuss their roles in your big day. This is the perfect time to set up a wedding budget, which will ultimately determine the size of wedding you will have. Ensure that all parties are clear on their roles and responsibilities to avoid problems in the future.

3. Should you hire a wedding consultant?

Consultants are individuals who specialize in wedding planning. They have an expansive knowledge base and can assist you in selecting the right vendors and in negotiating fees. They charge clients by the hour or establish a flat fee for services rendered. If you prefer to make the wedding arrangements yourself, you can also hire a consultant for your wedding day to handle any final payments and arrangements.

4. Is premarital counseling required?

Many churches ask engaged couples to fill out an "application" for marriage and attend several counseling sessions or classes with the minister who will officiate their wedding. These sessions cover a variety of topics ranging from wedding planning and the honeymoon to finances, raising children, sex and communication. In addition, you can expect the minister to ask you some personal questions regarding character traits, family traditions and beliefs, spirituality and life goals. This is done to ensure that both you and your intended have "covered your bases" and are ready to make a lifelong commitment to one another. Be sure to honestly answer each question the minister asks you.

5. Are there other requirements or details of which you should be aware?

Absolutely! There are literally hundreds of minute details that can be overlooked. To avoid making a costly mistake, purchase a wedding planner or wedding planner software. Most come equipped with spreadsheets, a timeline and checklists for the bride and groom. Keep in mind that marriage requirements and fees vary from state to state and county to county. U.S. residents who plan to wed abroad should check with the board of tourism or government at their destination for residency requirements and marriage license fees.

COUNTDOWN TO THE BIG DAY

Keep in mind that this checklist is not all-inclusive. To ensure that nothing is overlooked for your special day, talk to a Wedding Consultant, purchase a detailed planner or surf the Internet for assistance.

6 – 12 months before the wedding:

_____ Announce the engagement via e-mail, an engagement party, newspaper announcement or word-of-mouth.

_____ Set the date and choose the ceremony and reception sites (the availability of the latter two may determine the date of the wedding).

_____ Make an appointment with the minister and discuss the date of the wedding and requirements for marriage (i.e., counseling or classes).

_____ Discuss the budget and set it down on paper to keep you focused.

_____ Hire a wedding consultant or purchase a detailed planner.

_____ Create a notebook in which to place your wedding and honeymoon ideas, vendor contact numbers, contracts and a copy of your budget.

_____ Select your attendants, caterer, photographer, florist, DJ/band and videographer.

_____ Choose your wedding attire.

_____ Register for gifts at your favorite store.

3 – 6 months before:

_____ Begin premarital counseling (if necessary).
_____ Make final arrangements with vendors.
_____ Arrange for transportation.
_____ Begin to look for housing with your intended (if necsary).
_____ Create a guest list.

2 – 3 months before:

_____ Order the invitations and personal stationery.
_____ Order the flowers and cake.
_____ Purchase thank-you gifts for attendants.
_____ Plan the wedding rehearsal and dinner.
_____ Plan the ceremony with your minister.
_____ See your doctor for a complete physical exam and discuss birth control.
_____ If immunizations are necessary for the wedding or honeymoon, arrange to get them when you have your physical.
_____ Set up accommodations for out-of-town guests.
_____ Purchase wedding rings and have them engraved.
_____ Finalize honeymoon plans.

4 – 6 weeks before:

_____ Mail the invitations.
_____ Write thank-you notes as gifts arrive.
_____ Design your wedding program.
_____ Decide on wedding music.
_____ Purchase wedding accessories.
_____ Schedule a consultation with your hair and makeup stylists.

7 days before:

_____ Notify the caterer of the final number of guests.
_____ Go over final details with vendors.
_____ Confirm honeymoon arrangements and begin packing.
_____ Secure the marriage license with your intended.
_____ Make certain attendants have everything they need.
_____ Bride attends bridesmaids' luncheon; groom attends bachelor party/dinner.

The day before:

_____ Greet out-of-town guests as they arrive or arrange for their pick-up.
_____ Attend the rehearsal and dinner.
_____ Finish packing for the honeymoon.

Your Wedding Day:

_____ See your hair and makeup stylist for final beauty preparations.
_____ Relax and enjoy the day!

Exercise Twenty-Five:

HONEYMOON MAGIC

The honeymoon is a special time for a married couple to suspend everyday living in order to cement the bond between them. Complete the following statements and then read the list of helpful tips and suggestions provided to assist you in maximizing your time together.

1. This is where we plan to go for our honeymoon_____
   _____
   _____

2. I am looking forward to this time because_____
   _____
   _____

3. I am apprehensive because_____
   _____
   _____

4. What will I do if something goes amiss?_____
   _____
   _____

Destination Suggestions

Before setting your mind to a particular destination, research your options. You may be surprised at what is available!

- **All-Inclusive Resort:** These resorts offer combination wedding and honeymoon packages, in addition to a variety of honeymoon options. They are widely available in the Caribbean and Mexico in a range of budgets and accommodations.

- **Cruise:** Enjoy a plethora of destinations (and time frames) from your floating hotel.

- **Spa:** If you desire to unwind and be pampered during your honeymoon, check out the options at resorts or cruise ships with spas. Many offer special deals for honeymooners.

- **Villa:** Villas offer more privacy than a hotel and can come fully staffed. Rates vary from very expensive to moderate, with higher rates during peak vacation/tourist season. Many are located just a few feet from area attractions and beaches.

- **Adventure Trip:** If you have the time and the inclination to experience something a little more daring on your honeymoon, an adventure trip is for you! Destinations include Africa and the Australian Outback. Accommodations range from luxurious to inexpensive (such as a tent), with activities for every age and level of experience.

- **Hotel/Airline Package:** Many airlines offer fantastic hotel, car rental and airfare packages to a variety of overseas destinations, such as Great Britain, France and Italy. Hotels and resorts also offer specialty packages of their own, which often include golf, SCUBA diving or sightseeing tours. Visit their Web sites, if available, or speak to your travel agent.

ANSWER KEY

Exercise Eight: True Love or True Lust?

1) T   2) F   3) F   4) T   5) T   6) T   7) F   8) T   9) T   10) T
11) T   12) T   13) F

Exercise Sixteen: How Much Do You Really Know?

1) b   2) b   3) a   4) a   5) b   6) d   7) c   8) b   9) d   10) d

Exercise Seventeen: Test Your Knowledge

All of the answers are true, with the exception of number nine.

Exercise Twenty-Two: M.F.E.O. (Made for Each Other)

1) c   2) a   3) d   4) c   5) b   6) c   7) a   8) c   9) d   10) a

NOTES

NOTES

NOTES